HANDB

Dogs

Written by

Camilla de la Bedoyere

Miles Kelly

First published in 2015 by Miles Kelly Publishing Ltd
Harding's Barn, Bardfield End Green, Thaxted, Essex, CM6 3PX, UK

2 4 6 8 10 9 7 5 3 1

Publishing Director Belinda Gallagher
Creative Director Jo Cowan
Editorial Director Rosie Neave
Design Manager Simon Lee
Image Manager Liberty Newton
Production Manager Elizabeth Collins
Reprographics Stephan Davis, Jennifer Cozens, Thom Allaway

ISBN 978-1-78209-778-5

Printed in China

British Library Cataloguing-in-Publication Data
A catalogue record for this book is available from the British Library

ACKNOWLEDGEMENTS

All artworks are from the Miles Kelly Artwork Bank.

The publishers would like to thank the following sources for the use of their photographs:

Cover Jeanette Hutfluss/Tierfotoagentur/FLPA **Animals Animals** 58 Pearcy, Robert
Alamy 62 Tierfotoagentur; 86 epa european pressphoto agency b.v. **Corbis** 24 Stephen Barnes/Demotix; 46 Brock Miller **FLPA** 22 J.-L. Klein and M.-L. Hubert; 28 David Hosking;
40 Alexandra Pfau/Tierfotoagentur; 52 Justus de Cuveland/Imagebroker; 56 Kerstin Mielke/Tierfotoagentur;
74 Mitsuaki Iwago/Minden Pictures; 78 Wayne Hutchinson; 94 Dana Geithner/Tierfotoagentur
Glow 12 Yangfei Wu; 18 DLILLC/Corbis; 30 J. De Meester; 54 ARCO/Wegner, P.; 76 ARCO / Digoit, O.
NPL 38 Colin Seddon **Photoshot** 34 Xinhua; 66; 82 Tips; 88 NHPA; 90 Picture Alliance
Shutterstock 2 Zoonar GmbH; 4(cr) Jim DeLillo, (bl) Javier Brosch; 5(cl) Joca de Jong, (br) Debby Wong;
7(t to b) Jaromir Chalabala, Rita Kochmarjova, karelnoppe, Alexander Raths; 8(tl) CyberKat, (cr) Solovyova Lyudmyla;
9(cr) Makarova Viktoria, (bl) Liliya Kulianionak; 14 Zuzule; 16 Bildagentur Zoonar GmbH; 20 Degtyaryov Andrey;
26 Francois Loubser; 32 Rad Radu; 36 DragoNika; 42 Anna Tk; 44 Rita Kochmarjova; 48 SueC; 50 Denisa Doudova;
60 Gilles DeCruyenaere; 64 Tatiana Katsai; 68 Dora Zett; 70 Ruth Black; 72 Utekhina Anna; 80 cynoclub;
84 AnetaPics; 92 otsphoto

Every effort has been made to acknowledge the source and copyright holder of each picture.
Miles Kelly Publishing apologizes for any unintentional errors or omissions.

www.mileskelly.net
info@mileskelly.net

Contents

Checklist: Mark off the dogs you have seen in the tick boxes above.

What is a dog?

All around the world, dogs share their lives with humans. There are many different breeds of dog but they all belong to a single species within a much larger family of animals, called canids.

Wild ancestors

There are 36 different species of canids, which includes wolves, foxes, coyotes and jackals as well as the domestic dog. Pet dogs are probably all descended from wolves. Like their wild ancestors, dogs are clever, sociable animals. People first kept dogs as pets about 14,000 years ago.

Grey wolves live in large forests where they hunt other animals to eat. They live in family groups called packs.

It is in a dog's nature to be obedient and to trust its owner.

Living with people

Dogs are described as 'domesticated', which means that they live alongside humans and in their homes. They make good pets because they regard their owners as the leaders of their pack and try to please them.

Types of dog

Dog breeds can be organized into six main types. These types have been bred for their many qualities – how they look and behave.

TYPE	CHARACTERISTICS
Hounds	These dogs have been developed for hunting. Some of them hunt using sight, such as Greyhounds, while others use their sense of smell, such as Bloodhounds.
Gundogs	Gundogs were developed to follow hunters, find prey and retrieve birds or other animals that had been shot. They suit country life.
Terriers	These small dogs were bred to chase animals that run into burrows, such as badgers, rabbits, rats and foxes. They are usually clever, single-minded, active dogs.
Toy Dogs	Toy dogs tend to be very small. They have been bred to be family pets and companions. These dogs often suit town life and enjoy being with families.
Utility Dogs	These dogs come from mixed backgrounds and may have history of being both companion and working dogs. They are usually friendly and obedient.
Working Dogs	This is a large group of dog breeds. Working dogs are usually obedient and energetic. They are intelligent, so they can be trained, and are affectionate.

Pedigree, cross-breed or mongrel?

A pedigree dog is one that belongs to a particular breed, such as Chihuahua or Dalmatian. A female from one breed may be mated with a male from a different breed. The cross-bred puppies might have characteristics of both parents. A mongrel is a dog that has no obvious pedigree and may be descended from many types of dog.

A pedigree poodle takes part in a dog show.

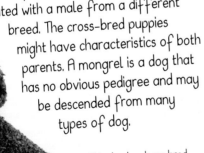

This dog has been bred from a labrador and a poodle. This cross-breed is sometimes known as a labradoodle.

Breeds

People have been breeding dogs for thousands of years, and new breeds are being developed all the time. Each breed has its own characteristics, but every dog is still an individual with its own personality.

Shape and size

A dog is described by its body shape and size, its colour, and the way it behaves. The shape of the head, muzzle, ears and tail are also used to distinguish breeds.

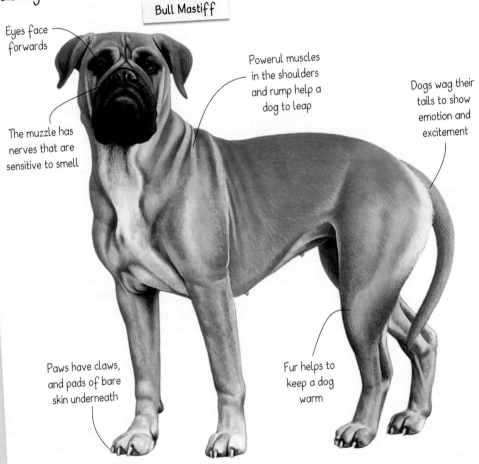

Bull Mastiff

Eyes face forwards

Powerul muscles in the shoulders and rump help a dog to leap

Dogs wag their tails to show emotion and excitement

The muzzle has nerves that are sensitive to smell

Paws have claws, and pads of bare skin underneath

Fur helps to keep a dog warm

Measuring dogs

Dogs are measured to their withers, which are the highest points of their shoulders. Most pedigree dogs that are entered into competitions are expected to fall into a 'perfect' size range, which might include weight as well as height. For family dogs, there is no perfect size. The sizes given in this book are a guide to the average size for a particular breed.

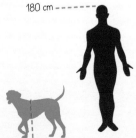

180 cm

Keeping healthy

It is a dog owner's responsibility to care for their pet, and keep their dog in tip-top condition so it can live a happy, healthy life.

Food Dogs need their own food – some human food is poisonous to them. They should be fed at least once a day and they must always have clean, fresh water.

Exercise Dogs need to run and walk every day to stay fit, but some breeds need more exercise than others. They like to play with dog-safe toys too.

Grooming Taking care of an animal's fur is called grooming. Some dogs like to be bathed, and others need regular brushing. Being stroked helps dogs to relax.

Visiting the vet Vets give owners the best advice for keeping their pet well. Their special care will help to keep a dog free from diseases and parasites (such as worms). They also neuter dogs, so they can't have puppies.

Looking out for health issues

Here are some common problems to look out for. A vet can treat your dog for all these ailments.

HEALTH ISSUE	WHAT TO DO
Fleas	Fleas are jumping insects that irritate a dog by biting its skin and sucking blood. Most dogs get fleas at some time in their lives.
Vomiting	Dogs are often sick because they like to eat things they shouldn't! However, vomiting can also be a sign of a serious illness.
Coughing	Dogs can catch viruses just like humans. A nasty cough, runny nose and weeping eyes may mean that a dog has kennel cough.
Ear mites	Ear mites are tiny bugs that make a dog's ears itchy, causing it distress. Dogs with ear mites often scratch their ears and shake their heads.

Dog behaviour

Like their wild cousins, dogs are intelligent animals that like to explore their world. They are sociable, which means they need company. Dogs should be trained to behave well and follow orders.

Dogs have a much better sense of smell than humans.

A dog's life

Dogs are curious animals that like to sniff at everything. They also enjoy chewing, chasing, playing fetch and visiting new places. Dogs lead busy lives so they can get tired quickly and enjoy naps in the day.

To help a puppy learn basic commands such as sit, stay, down and no, a small reward may be given if they follow instructions.

Training a dog

It is important that dogs begin their training when they are still puppies. During training they learn to do as they are told, so they do not pose a danger to other animals or people.

Training tips

O Take your puppy to dog training classes so you and your pet can learn how to understand and trust each other.

O Dogs should be rewarded for good behaviour, not punished for bad behaviour.

O Learn about dog behaviour so you can spot signs of stress, boredom and fear in your pet.

Golden rules

Dogs are animals, and like all animals they can sometimes behave in a way we do not like or did not expect. It is important to remember that even gentle dogs can sometimes be aggressive and may bite or scare people.

- Never grab, tease or hit a dog. Do not pull its tail or try to climb on to it. Always be kind to animals.
- Never go up to a dog you don't know.
- Do not disturb a dog that is eating or sleeping, playing with a toy, or is unwell.
- Make sure your dog has somewhere quiet it can go to when it is tired or unhappy.

- If a dog is scared it is may try to defend itself, so keep it away from frightening situations such as fireworks or railways.
- A child should never be left alone in a room with a dog, even a dog that the child knows.

Being a good dog owner

Good dog owners understand that they are responsible for their pet, its happiness, health and its behaviour. That means they must clear up a dog's mess, keep it on a lead and make sure other people and animals are always safe around the dog.

Dogs can scare farm animals, and must be kept under control at all times.

Mother dogs care for their puppies, feeding them with milk as they grow.

Mothers and pups

Taking care of a pregnant dog is a special job, and owners should ask for help and advice from their vet. When a dog gives birth she is said to be 'whelping'.
Newborn puppies are blind and helpless, and should stay with their mother until they are about ten weeks old.

How to use this book

Dogs are special animals that have earned a place in our hearts and homes. By filling in the pages of this book you will learn how to recognize 42 different breeds. There are spaces for your notes, sketches and photos.

Photofile

This photo may show the breed in action, as a puppy, in a different colourway, or a different but related breed, and is accompanied by extra information.

My observations

Start by writing down the date of your sighting. Then make a note of any colours and markings. Is it an older dog or a young puppy? Notice how the dog behaves. Is its tail wagging? Is it sniffing or barking?

My drawings and photos

Fill these spaces with your sketches and photographs.

Photos

Take photos of dogs that belong to friends and family. Have your camera ready – dogs move fast, so you have to be prepared! Natural light will give you the best pictures. Experiment with different angles and see what works best.

Drawings

Use a soft pencil, such as 2B, because the lead is easy to rub out. Look carefully at the dog's body and head shape. Add arrows with labels such as 'small, pointed ears' and 'long, fluffy fur'. You don't always need to draw the whole dog – try just sketching the head.

MY OBSERVATIONS

Date:

Age (if known):

Colour of fur:

Special markings/features:

Behaviour:

A Bulldog's lower jaw juts forward, coming in front of the upper jaw. This mouth shape was useful when the breed was used to fight bears, as dogs attack bears from below.

MY DRAWINGS AND PHOTOS

I saw this dog: at home   in a park

64

Where?

Tick one of the boxes on the location bar to record where you had your sighting.

Main text
Every right-hand page
has a main paragraph
to introduce each breed.

Scale guide
Each breed in this book is compared
against a silhouette of a person. This
will help you to understand how big
or small it actually is.

Colour coding
The entries in this book are organized
into sections. Each section covers breeds
belonging to one of six different types
of dog. The pages of each section are
colour-coded, making it easy to find the
breed you have spotted.

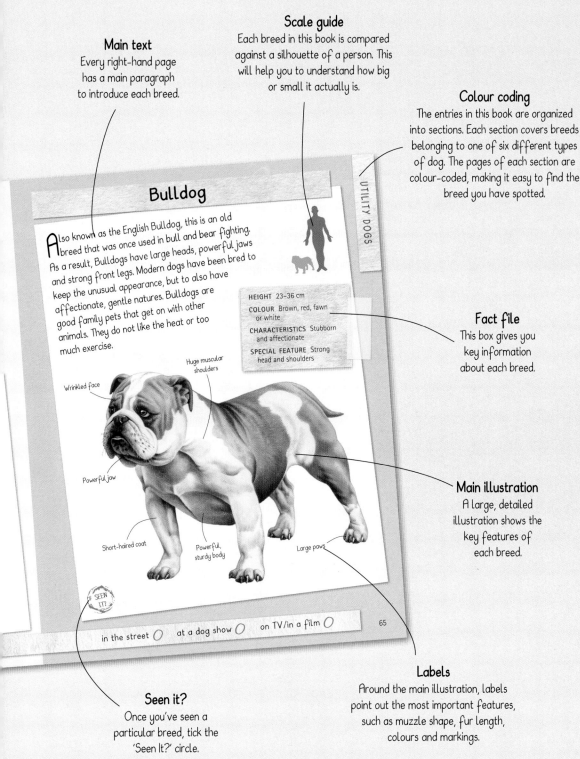

Bulldog

UTILITY DOGS

Also known as the English Bulldog, this is an old
breed that was once used in bull and bear fighting.
As a result, Bulldogs have large heads, powerful jaws
and strong front legs. Modern dogs have been bred to
keep the unusual appearance, but to also have
affectionate, gentle natures. Bulldogs are
good family pets that get on with other
animals. They do not like the heat or too
much exercise.

HEIGHT 23–36 cm
COLOUR Brown, red, fawn
or white
CHARACTERISTICS Stubborn
and affectionate
SPECIAL FEATURE Strong
head and shoulders

Fact file
This box gives you
key information
about each breed.

Huge muscular
shoulders

Wrinkled face

Powerful jaw

Main illustration
A large, detailed
illustration shows the
key features of
each breed.

Short-haired coat

Powerful,
sturdy body

Large paws

SEEN
IT?

in the street ◯   at a dog show ◯   on TV/in a film ◯   65

Seen it?
Once you've seen a
particular breed, tick the
'Seen It?' circle.

Labels
Around the main illustration, labels
point out the most important features,
such as muzzle shape, fur length,
colours and markings.

11

MY OBSERVATIONS

Date:

Age (if known):

Colour of fur:

Special markings/features:

Behaviour:

Afghans are a type of sight hound, which means that they hunt using speed and sight, rather than their sense of smell, to track another animal.

MY DRAWINGS AND PHOTOS

I saw this dog: at home ◯   in a park ◯

Afghan

This ancient breed was once used for hunting. Afghan hounds combine strength, speed and stubbornness. They have a distinctive body shape with long, lean legs and expressive eyes. Afghan fur grows long and silky and needs regular grooming to stay in top condition. Although these hounds may behave coolly towards strangers, they are very loyal to their owners. Afghans can be difficult to train.

HEIGHT 63–74 cm

COLOUR Black, brown, red, white, tan, blue, grey and mixed colours

CHARACTERISTICS Shy and loyal

SPECIAL FEATURE Long, silky fur

Small head is held high

Well-muscled shoulders

Elegant, athletic body

Tail is set low

Coat has patches of different colour

Paws are covered by fur

Silky coat with long fur

SEEN IT?

in the street ◯   at a dog show ◯   on TV/in a film ◯

MY OBSERVATIONS

Date:

Age (if known):

Colour of fur:

Special markings/features:

Behaviour:

Even a Basset hound puppy has folds of skin around its face and neck. This breed has droopy eyes, and Bassets often seem to have a sad expression.

MY DRAWINGS AND PHOTOS

I saw this dog: at home ◯   in a park ◯

Basset

These hounds have large, heavy bodies on short legs. Bassets were originally bred to hunt hares and they have an extremely good sense of smell. They have independent minds, which can make them difficult to train. However, Bassets like company and enjoy playing. They can be noisy and may bark loudly if worried, lonely or excited. Bassets sometimes have problems with their hearing and the joints in their legs.

HEIGHT 33–38 cm

COLOUR Black, tan and white

CHARACTERISTICS Playful and friendly

SPECIAL FEATURE Stumpy legs

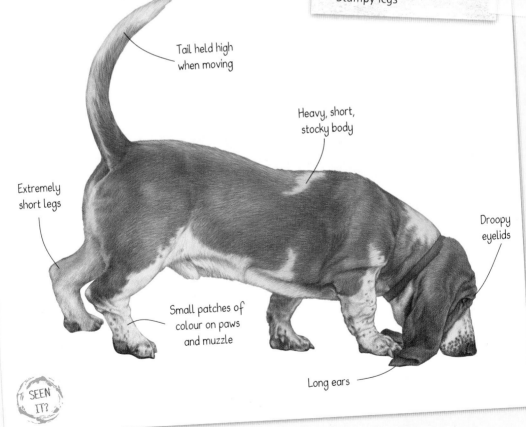

Tail held high when moving

Heavy, short, stocky body

Extremely short legs

Droopy eyelids

Small patches of colour on paws and muzzle

Long ears

SEEN IT?

MY OBSERVATIONS

Date:

Age (if known):

Colour of fur:

Special markings/features:

Behaviour:

English Foxhounds look similar to Beagles, but are taller, with average heights of 60 cm. They are strong, tireless and stubborn dogs, so they are not ideal family pets.

MY DRAWINGS AND PHOTOS

I saw this dog: at home ◯   in a park ◯

Beagle

Like other hounds, Beagles are active, energetic dogs with good appetites. They can be difficult to train, especially if they have developed bad habits. Beagles are intelligent, enjoy being around people and are loyal to their owners. They have a good sense of smell and enjoy sniffing everything.

HEIGHT 33–40 cm

COLOUR Black, tan and white

CHARACTERISTICS Sociable and good-natured

SPECIAL FEATURE Energetic hunter

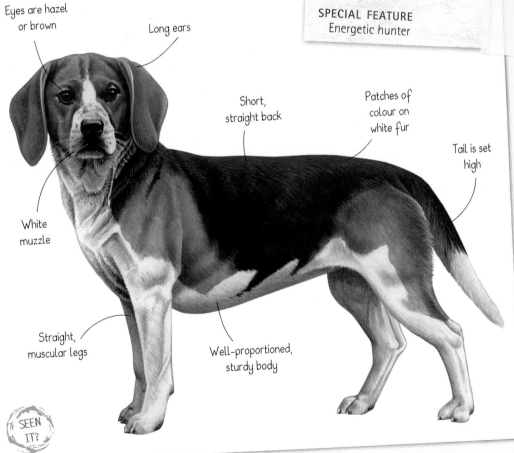

Eyes are hazel or brown

Long ears

Short, straight back

Patches of colour on white fur

Tail is set high

White muzzle

Straight, muscular legs

Well-proportioned, sturdy body

SEEN IT?

MY OBSERVATIONS

Date:

Age (if known):

Colour of fur:

Special markings/features:

Behaviour:

MY DRAWINGS AND PHOTOS

A Bloodhound's muzzle contains up to 40 times as many smell cells as a human's nose. This dog can pick up a scent trail using clues such as sweat, breath or blood.

I saw this dog: at home ◯   in a park ◯

Bloodhound

Despite their name and size, Bloodhounds are sweet-natured, loving dogs. They have a superb sense of smell, which is why they are used for tracking. Bloodhounds need plenty of food to support their large bodies, but they should only eat small, regular meals to prevent a painful stomach disorder. These large hounds are friendly and enjoy playing. Training takes patience and time.

HEIGHT 58–69 cm

COLOUR Tan

CHARACTERISTICS Gentle and patient

SPECIAL FEATURE Superb sense of smell

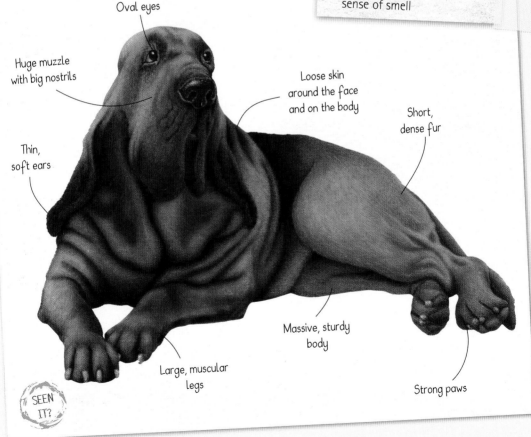

Oval eyes

Huge muzzle with big nostrils

Loose skin around the face and on the body

Short, dense fur

Thin, soft ears

Massive, sturdy body

Strong paws

Large, muscular legs

SEEN IT?

in the street ◯   at a dog show ◯   on TV/in a film ◯

MY OBSERVATIONS

Date: _____

Age (if known): _____

Colour of fur: _____

_____

Special markings/features: _____

_____

_____

Behaviour: _____

_____

_____

Borzois have a long, narrow muzzle because they are bred from greyhounds. Their alert eyes face forwards, helping them to hunt using eyesight rather than smell.

MY DRAWINGS AND PHOTOS

I saw this dog: at home ◯   in a park ◯

Borzoi

Also known as Russian Wolfhounds, Borzois are suited to chasing and catching other animals. They have long, powerful jaws and lean, muscular legs. Although Borzois can be friendly and good-natured, as hounds they may be wilful and less eager to please humans than some breeds. This means they can be difficult to train for obedience.

HEIGHT 68–74 cm

COLOUR Various including gold, grey and red

CHARACTERISTICS Stubborn and calm

SPECIAL FEATURE Fast runner

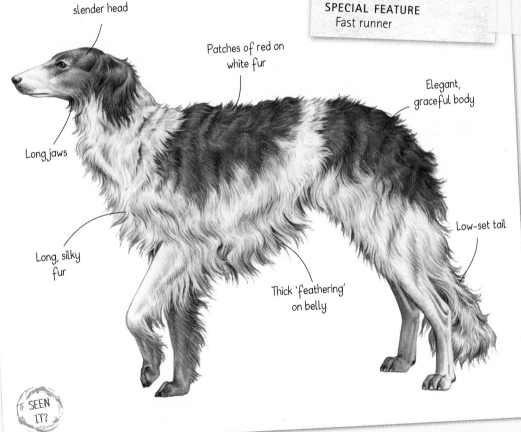

Small, slender head

Patches of red on white fur

Elegant, graceful body

Long jaws

Long, silky fur

Thick 'feathering' on belly

Low-set tail

SEEN IT?

MY OBSERVATIONS

Date:

Age (if known):

Colour of fur:

Special markings/features:

Behaviour:

Wire-haired Dachshunds have short, rough hair, a thick undercoat, beards and long-haired eyebrows. They are more active than their short-haired cousins.

MY DRAWINGS AND PHOTOS

I saw this dog: at home ◯   in a park ◯

Dachshund

These hounds are small in height, but big in personality. Dachshunds were bred as hunting dogs, as their long, low bodies were ideal for chasing prey into tunnels. Today, they are popular family pets because they are loyal and intelligent. Dachshunds need to learn how to behave around children and other animals from an early age. They can be difficult to train and are sometimes unfriendly to strangers.

WEIGHT 9–12 kg (these dogs are not measured in height)

COLOUR Brown, or black and tan

CHARACTERISTICS Clever and bossy

SPECIAL FEATURE Short legs

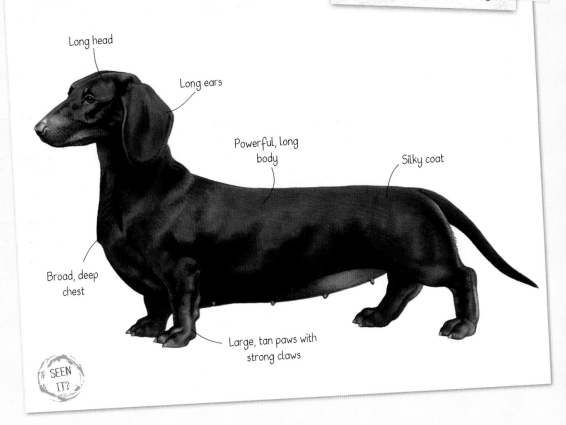

Long head

Long ears

Powerful, long body

Silky coat

Broad, deep chest

Large, tan paws with strong claws

SEEN IT?

MY OBSERVATIONS

Date:

Age (if known):

Colour of fur:

Special markings/features:

Behaviour:

The Irish Guards have had an Irish Wolfhound as their mascot for more than 100 years. The dog leads the regiment on all parades, and wears its own 'uniform'.

MY DRAWINGS AND PHOTOS

I saw this dog: at home ◯   in a park ◯

Irish Wolfhound

This is one of the largest breeds of dog and also one of the gentlest. Irish Wolfhounds were first bred to hunt wolves and other large animals. However, those early dogs probably did not reach the great sizes seen today. These hounds are affectionate, but can be difficult to look after because of their size.

HEIGHT 71–79 cm

COLOUR Grey, red, black, white or fawn

CHARACTERISTICS Gentle and calm

SPECIAL FEATURE Huge size

Large head

Small, dark eyes

Small ears

Long neck

Long muzzle

Powerful, muscular body

Long tail

Deep chest

Muscular legs with large paws

Shaggy fur

SEEN IT?

in the street ○   at a dog show ○   on TV/in a film ○

MY OBSERVATIONS

Date: _____

Age (if known): _____

Colour of fur: _____

_____

Special markings/features: _____

_____

_____

Behaviour: _____

_____

_____

Whippets were originally bred from Greyhounds that were too small to hunt. Today, Greyhounds love to run and they are the fastest of all dogs.

MY DRAWINGS AND PHOTOS

I saw this dog: at home ◯   in a park ◯

Whippet

These dogs are one of the friendliest and most loyal of all hounds. Whippets have patient natures and quickly learn to adore their owners. They are fast runners and love to hunt. Curious, alert and active, whippets are always on the lookout for something to chase. Whippets are sometimes known as 'Snapdogs' because they can kill a rat with a single snap of their jaws.

HEIGHT 44–51 cm

COLOUR Black, brown, red, white, tan, blue, grey and mixed colours

CHARACTERISTICS
Intelligent and patient

SPECIAL FEATURE
Small but fast

Long, thin muzzle

Elegant, slender body is graceful and muscular

Small paws

Slender tail

SEEN IT?

MY OBSERVATIONS

Date:

Age (if known):

Colour of fur:

Special markings/features:

Behaviour:

An English Cocker Spaniel is an active dog that needs plenty of exercise. These dogs have a powerful instinct to retrieve (bring things back for their owners).

MY DRAWINGS AND PHOTOS

I saw this dog: at home ◯   in a park ◯

English Cocker Spaniel

These curious, active dogs love to sniff and explore. English Cocker Spaniels were originally bred to accompany hunters and find birds or other animals that had been shot. They are friendly family pets that love to be kept busy, especially by catching, fetching and playing. Cocker Spaniels have silky fur, which grows long around their legs, so they need to be groomed regularly.

HEIGHT 38–41 cm

COLOUR Orange or black

CHARACTERISTICS Charming and companionable

SPECIAL FEATURE Loves to carry things

Large, brown eyes

White patches in coat

Compact, medium-sized body

Tail set low

Long ears

Strong back legs

Silky fur

Long fur around the legs

SEEN IT?

MY OBSERVATIONS

Date:
_____

Age (if known):
_____

Colour of fur:
_____
_____

Special markings/features:
_____
_____
_____

Behaviour:
_____
_____
_____

Assistance dogs help people with everyday tasks that they find difficult. The dogs begin their training as puppies, and the training takes more than a year.

MY DRAWINGS AND PHOTOS

I saw this dog: at home ◯   in a park ◯

Golden Retriever

Popular and loveable, these dogs were first bred from Spaniels, Labrador Retrievers and Red Setters. Golden Retrievers have developed into a breed of reliable, intelligent and trusting dogs. Obedient and quick to learn, they are often used as working dogs, especially assistance dogs. Golden Retrievers are known for their gentle natures, so they are especially popular as family pets. They love to play, fetch and chew, and also enjoy swimming.

HEIGHT 52–61 cm

COLOUR Cream or golden

CHARACTERISTICS Obedient and intelligent

SPECIAL FEATURE Works as an assistance dog

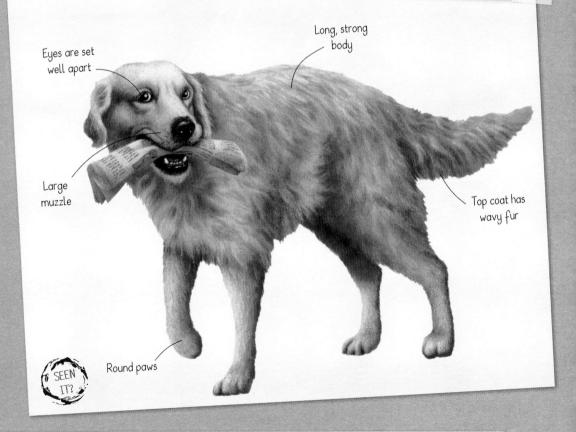

Long, strong body

Eyes are set well apart

Large muzzle

Top coat has wavy fur

Round paws

SEEN IT?

MY OBSERVATIONS

Date: _____

Age (if known): _____

Colour of fur: _____
_____

Special markings/features: _____
_____
_____

Behaviour: _____
_____
_____

When an Irish Setter smells something interesting it adopts this 'pointer' position. The dog stands still, giving its owner time to come close and investigate.

MY DRAWINGS AND PHOTOS

I saw this dog: at home ◯   in a park ◯

Irish Setter

First bred as hunting dogs, Irish Setters have an excellent sense of smell. They are known for their great beauty and elegance. Their chestnut coat can be groomed until it shines and is silky to the touch. Irish Setters are energetic and easily distracted. They love to chase and sniff, but it can be difficult to get them to return when called, so training is important.

HEIGHT 61–65 cm

COLOUR Chestnut

CHARACTERISTICS
Enthusiastic and affectionate

SPECIAL FEATURE
A beautiful coat

Almond-shaped
eyes

Elegant, slender
head

Muscular, graceful
body

Long jaws

Strong legs

Long, silky fur

MY OBSERVATIONS

Date:
_____

Age (if known):
_____

Colour of fur:
_____
_____

Special markings/features:
_____
_____
_____

Behaviour:
_____
_____
_____

Labrador Retrievers make good detection, or sniffer, dogs so they are often hard at work in airports. They can be trained to sniff out drugs, explosives and even mobile phones!

MY DRAWINGS AND PHOTOS

I saw this dog: at home ◯   in a park ◯

Labrador Retriever

The first Labrador Retrievers worked with hunters and fishermen. Friendly and highly intelligent, they have become popular family pets. These dogs can be trained and are obedient. They work as trackers with the police, or as assistance dogs. Labrador Retrievers enjoy any chance to swim or fetch balls from a pond. Their coats are waterproof, so they do not mind getting wet.

HEIGHT 54–57 cm

COLOUR Black, chocolate or yellow

CHARACTERISTICS Sociable and affectionate

SPECIAL FEATURE Loves water

Intelligent expression

Sloping shoulders

Chocolate-coloured coat

Large muzzle

Tail is thick at the base

Short, dense fur

Sporty, solid body

Round paws

SEEN IT?

MY OBSERVATIONS

Date:
_____

Age (if known):
_____

Colour of fur:
_____

_____

Special markings/features:
_____

_____

Behaviour:
_____

_____

Weimaraner puppies are bright and curious. One of their favourite pastimes is chewing, so they need to be given plenty of chewy toys.

MY DRAWINGS AND PHOTOS

I saw this dog: at home ◯   in a park ◯

Weimaraner

Developed in Germany, Weimaraners were once popular as hunting dogs. Today they are kept as pets and show dogs, because they have a good nature and an unusual appearance. They are sometimes called 'grey ghosts', because of the strange but beautiful grey-brown colour of their coats. Weimaraners are friendly dogs, but they bark at strangers, which makes them good guard dogs.

HEIGHT 56–69 cm

COLOUR Grey

CHARACTERISTICS Energetic and sharp

SPECIAL FEATURE Eyes are blue or amber in colour

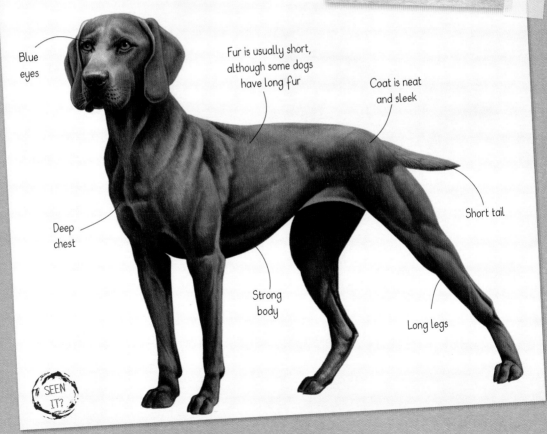

Blue eyes

Fur is usually short, although some dogs have long fur

Coat is neat and sleek

Deep chest

Short tail

Strong body

Long legs

SEEN IT?

MY OBSERVATIONS

Date:

Age (if known):

Colour of fur:

Special markings/features:

Behaviour:

Some farmers keep Border Terriers to help them control farmyard pests. If a Border Terrier sees a rat or rabbit it may try to follow it into its burrow!

MY DRAWINGS AND PHOTOS

I saw this dog: at home ◯   in a park ◯

Border Terrier

Terriers were first bred to accompany hunters and chase or catch animals. Border Terriers were fast runners, but they were also small enough to chase foxes down their holes. Today, Border Terriers are kept as family pets. They love to play and are good companions for children. Border Terriers are obedient, but need firm training as they have lively spirits.

HEIGHT 28–30 cm

COLOUR Red, brown, fawn and tan

CHARACTERISTICS Good-natured

SPECIAL FEATURE Strong hunting instinct

Rounded head

Ears, muzzle and eyes are usually dark

Moustache

Long, wiry fur feels rough

Sturdy, active body

Strong claws

SEEN IT?

MY OBSERVATIONS

Date:

Age (if known):

Colour of fur:

Special markings/features:

Behaviour:

These terriers have strong jaws and a sharp bite. They have high spirits with a strong hunting instinct, so should be kept away from small animals.

MY DRAWINGS AND PHOTOS

I saw this dog: at home ◯   in a park ◯

Parson Russell Terrier

Parson Russell Terriers are descended from Fox Terriers. They were bred by a parson called Reverend John Russell. He wanted a dog that could chase a fox into a hole, but with legs long enough to run beside a horse. A popular breed ever since, these dogs are intelligent, but need firm training. They must spend time with people when they are young to become patient, calm and obedient.

HEIGHT 28–38 cm

COLOUR White with lemon, tan or black markings

CHARACTERISTICS Stubborn and affectionate

SPECIAL FEATURE Loves to dig

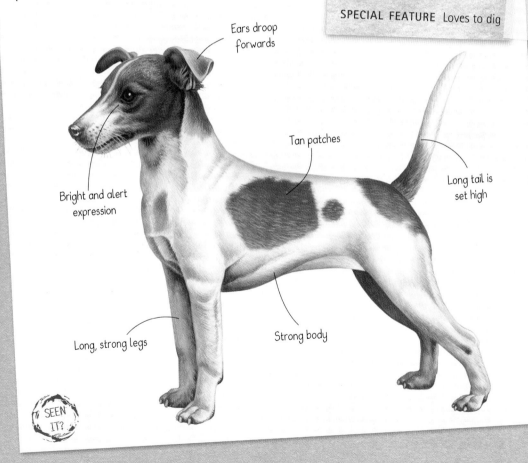

Ears droop forwards

Tan patches

Long tail is set high

Bright and alert expression

Long, strong legs

Strong body

SEEN IT?

MY OBSERVATIONS

Date:
_____

Age (if known):
_____

Colour of fur:
_____

_____

Special markings/features:
_____

_____

_____

Behaviour:
_____

_____

_____

A cream-coloured Scottie is described as 'wheaten' and even black Scotties may have white chests. A Scottie's coat has a rough topcoat and a soft undercoat.

MY DRAWINGS AND PHOTOS

I saw this dog: at home ◯   in a park ◯

Scottish Terrier

These Terriers are also known as Scottie Dogs. They are usually black, although other colours do exist. Scottish Terriers are surprisingly bold for their size and, like other terriers, they can be stubborn. They have a sweet appearance, but sometimes have short tempers and do not like being teased. Scottish Terriers are intelligent and loyal to their owners, but can be difficult to train.

HEIGHT 25–28 cm

COLOUR Black

CHARACTERISTICS Friendly and fearless

SPECIAL FEATURE Skilled at catching rats

Long-haired eyebrows

Tall ears

Long neck

Solid, thick-set body

Thick tail is held upright

Wiry coat

Long fur on the muzzle and legs

Short legs

SEEN IT?

in the street ◯   at a dog show ◯   on TV/in a film ◯

MY OBSERVATIONS

Date:

Age (if known):

Colour of fur:

Special markings/features:

Behaviour:

When a dog's fur has flecks of pale colour running through the dark base colour it is described as 'brindle'. Many Staffordshire Bull Terriers have brindle coats.

MY DRAWINGS AND PHOTOS

I saw this dog: at home $\bigcirc$ in a park $\bigcirc$

Staffordshire Bull Terrier

Staffies, as they are often known, belong to an English breed that was developed by mixing bulldogs and terriers. They have been bred to be incredibly powerful dogs and were once used for dog-fighting and catching rats, but now they are popular pets. Affectionate and loving, staffies can be stubborn and do not get on well with other dogs. They need firm training and lots of exercise.

HEIGHT 35–41 cm

COLOUR Fawn, red, brown or black

CHARACTERISTICS Boisterous and bold

SPECIAL FEATURE Strength

Large cheek muscles

Solid, muscular, powerful body

Straight tail

Large, square-shaped head

Short, smooth coat

SEEN IT?

MY OBSERVATIONS

Date:
_____

Age (if known):
_____

Colour of fur:
_____

_____

Special markings/features:
_____

_____

_____

Behaviour:
_____

_____

_____

The coats of Wire Fox Terriers kept for show are hand stripped. This means that any dead outer hair is pulled out by hand rather than clipped, to avoid dulling the fur's colour and softening its texture.

MY DRAWINGS AND PHOTOS

I saw this dog: at home ◯   in a park ◯

Wire Fox Terrier

Most Terriers tend to be stubborn and the Wire Fox Terrier is no exception. Terriers were bred to fix their attention on their prey, so they are not easily distracted. Wire Fox Terriers have lots of energy and personality. If they are used to being with children from a young age, they become very sociable and patient. They like to play and love to dig.

HEIGHT 39 cm maximum

COLOUR White or tan with black markings

CHARACTERISTICS Brave and sociable

SPECIAL FEATURE Healthy and long-lived

Small, dark eyes

Narrow, rectangular head

Square, firm body

White fur with patches

Long fur on the muzzle and legs

Thick coat

SEEN IT?

MY OBSERVATIONS

Date:
_____

Age (if known):
_____

Colour of fur:
_____
_____

Special markings/features:
_____
_____
_____

Behaviour:
_____
_____
_____

The fur of a Bichon Frise is soft to the touch and its ears are almost hidden by hair. This dog is descended from the Poodle and a type of fluffy spaniel.

MY DRAWINGS AND PHOTOS

I saw this dog: at home ◯   in a park ◯

Bichon Frise

Little Bichon Frise dogs are always white and have thick, fluffy coats. They are kept as companion dogs, but are also popular as show dogs. These dogs require grooming to keep their fur in top condition. Their coat can either be allowed to grow long and curly, or trimmed short. Good-natured, these dogs make perfect pets for caring children and they do not need much exercise.

HEIGHT 23–28 cm

COLOUR White

CHARACTERISTICS Happy and lively

SPECIAL FEATURE Thick white coat

Ears covered in long hair

Raised, curved tail

Rounded head with a strong jaw

Small, rounded paws

Small, solid, square-shaped body

SEEN IT?

MY OBSERVATIONS

Date:

Age (if known):

Colour of fur:

Special markings/features:

Behaviour:

A dog with three colours is described as a 'tricolour'. The spaniel on the right is a black, white and tan tricolour. The colour of the spaniel on the left is described as 'ruby'.

MY DRAWINGS AND PHOTOS

I saw this dog: at home ◯   in a park ◯

Cavalier King Charles Spaniel

These charming little dogs are named after an English King, Charles II, who loved the breed. They are similar to King Charles Spaniels, although slightly larger and less snub-nosed. Easy to train, simple to care for and eager to please, Cavalier King Charles Spaniels make good family pets and are welcoming to strangers.

HEIGHT Around 32 cm

COLOUR White and tan, black and tan, black

CHARACTERISTICS Easy-going and affectionate

SPECIAL FEATURE Long, feathery ears

Large eyes with gentle expression

Straight back

Patches of tan fur

Furry tail

Long ears

Elegant, athletic body

Long, silky fur, especially around the legs

SEEN IT?

MY OBSERVATIONS

Date: _____

Age (if known): _____

Colour of fur: _____

_____

Special markings/features: _____

_____

_____

Behaviour: _____

_____

_____

Chihuahuas need to be walked every day, even though they do not like the cold. Owners can address this problem by dressing their dogs in cosy winter coats.

MY DRAWINGS AND PHOTOS

I saw this dog: at home ◯   in a park ◯

Chihuahua

It is thought that modern Chihuahuas are descended from an older South or Central American breed of tiny dog. They are one of the smallest breeds, but they have big personalities and are brave and friendly. Chihuahuas have small appetites and need several small meals throughout the day. If they are looked after well, Chihuahuas can live longer than most dogs and may reach 20 years of age.

HEIGHT 15–23 cm

COLOUR Black, brown, red, tan, fawn, grey and white

CHARACTERISTICS Spirited

SPECIAL FEATURE Very long-lived

Small, domed head

Large ears

Attractive face with large eyes

Tail held high when moving

Small, sturdy body

Long-haired coat

Dainty paws

SEEN IT?

in the street ◯   at a dog show ◯   on TV/in a film ◯

MY OBSERVATIONS

Date:

Age (if known):

Colour of fur:

Special markings/features:

Behaviour:

A Powderpuff Chinese Crested Dog can be born in the same litter as a hairless one. Hairless dogs must be bathed regularly and Powderpuffs need daily grooming.

MY DRAWINGS AND PHOTOS

I saw this dog: at home ◯   in a park ◯

Chinese Crested Dog

There are two types of Chinese Crested Dogs. One type is hairless, except for the hair on its head, neck, tail and feet. The other type has long, soft hair all over its body and is called a Powderpuff. Both types of dog have a contented nature and are easy to look after. They are happy to exercise by playing in the garden and enjoy being with children.

HEIGHT 23–33 cm

COLOUR Usually white or silvery white

CHARACTERISTICS Cheerful and sociable

SPECIAL FEATURE Hairless

Large ears

Hairless skin

Fine hair on the head and neck

Tail has hair

Patches of colour on the skin

Hairy feet

MY OBSERVATIONS

Date:

Age (if known):

Colour of fur:

Special markings/features:

Behaviour:

A Papillon is keen to please, which makes it a fast learner. These dogs perform well at agility shows, and enjoy tasks such as racing between slalom poles.

MY DRAWINGS AND PHOTOS

I saw this dog: at home ◯   in a park ◯

Papillon

Little Papillon dogs are named after the French word for butterfly, because their large ears look like butterfly wings. They are usually kept as companion dogs or to show at competitions, but some Papillons also work as assistance dogs. This is an old breed and Papillons were once popular with royal families of Europe. Today, they make good family pets, being friendly, clever, obedient and loving.

HEIGHT 20–28 cm

COLOUR White with patches of colour

CHARACTERISTICS Alert and active

SPECIAL FEATURE Large ears

Large, feathery ears look like butterfly wings

A blaze of white on the forehead looks like a butterfly's body

Small, delicate face

Dainty, delicate body

Furry tail

Long, silky fur

SEEN IT?

MY OBSERVATIONS

Date:
_____

Age (if known):
_____

Colour of fur:
_____
_____

Special markings/features:
_____
_____
_____

Behaviour:
_____
_____
_____

Trimming a Pekingese's long fur gives a dog the chance to explore and play like other dogs. A haircut also helps the animal to keep cool in hot weather.

MY DRAWINGS AND PHOTOS

I saw this dog: at home ◯   in a park ◯

Pekingese

These dogs are named after the Chinese city of Beijing, which was once known as Peking. Pekes, as they are often called, were kept by the Chinese royal family and ordinary people were forbidden to own one. Eventually, some Pekes were taken out of China and one was presented to British Queen Victoria. Pekes are well-mannered and like being with families. They do not particularly enjoy exercising and prefer walking to running.

HEIGHT 18 cm

COLOUR Black, brown, red, tan, fawn, grey and white

CHARACTERISTICS Aloof and faithful

SPECIAL FEATURE Thick coat of long fur

Compact, furry body

Large, wide, rounded head

Flat face

Long, fluffy tail curls over the back

Short, thick neck

Large paws

SEEN IT?

MY OBSERVATIONS

Date:

Age (if known):

Colour of fur:

Special markings/features:

Behaviour:

Pomeranian puppies are unusually small and delicate at birth. Up to three puppies are usually born in a litter, although litters of up to seven puppies do occur.

MY DRAWINGS AND PHOTOS

I saw this dog: at home ◯   in a park ◯

Pomeranian

Little Pomeranians need a great deal of grooming. Thankfully, these companion dogs enjoy plenty of attention. Probably descended from the larger working Spitz breed that pulled sleds in the Arctic region, Pomeranians are energetic but do not need a lot of exercise. They are intelligent and fairly easy to train, but they have to learn to control their desire to yap.

HEIGHT 22–28 cm

COLOUR Orange, black or white

CHARACTERISTICS Bouncy and yappy

SPECIAL FEATURE Fox-like face

Fox-like face

Long, fluffy tail is held over the body

Fur has a thick undercoat

Short neck

Fragile, compact, miniature body

Fine-boned legs with small paws

SEEN IT?

MY OBSERVATIONS

Date:
_____

Age (if known):
_____

Colour of fur:
_____
_____

Special markings/features:
_____
_____
_____

Behaviour:
_____
_____
_____

The Biewer Yorkshire Terrier is a new breed of long-haired Toy Yorkie with a tricolour coat. The three colours are usually white, black and tan. Biewers are good family dogs.

MY DRAWINGS AND PHOTOS

I saw this dog: at home O in a park O

Yorkshire Terrier

Often known as Yorkies, these dogs are popular as companions and show dogs. They have incredible coats of long, silky fur. Yorkshire Terriers are probably descended from a mixture of terrier breeds, and developed into very small dogs with long fur. They are clever and brave. Despite their size, Yorkshire Terriers will attack dogs much larger than themselves. They are not always patient with children.

HEIGHT 18–20 cm

COLOUR Steel blue and bright tan

CHARACTERISTICS Aloof and intelligent

SPECIAL FEATURE Long, silky fur

A band or ribbon can be used to keep fur out of the dog's eyes

Tall, alert ears

Straight back

Steel blue fur

Short muzzle

Tan fur is dark at the roots, but light at the tips

Fur on body is long and glossy

SEEN IT?

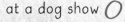

MY OBSERVATIONS

Date: _____

Age (if known): _____

Colour of fur: _____

_____

Special markings/features: _____

_____

_____

Behaviour: _____

_____

_____

A Bulldog's lower jaw juts forward, coming in front of the upper jaw. This mouth shape was useful when the breed was used to fight bears, as dogs attack bears from below.

MY DRAWINGS AND PHOTOS

I saw this dog: at home ◯   in a park ◯

Bulldog

Also known as the English Bulldog, this is an old breed that was once used in bull and bear fighting. As a result, Bulldogs have large heads, powerful jaws and strong front legs. Modern dogs have been bred to keep the unusual appearance, but to also have affectionate, gentle natures. Bulldogs are good family pets that get on with other animals. They do not like the heat or too much exercise.

HEIGHT 23–36 cm

COLOUR Brown, red, fawn or white

CHARACTERISTICS Stubborn and affectionate

SPECIAL FEATURE Strong head and shoulders

Wrinkled face

Huge muscular shoulders

Powerful jaw

Short-haired coat

Powerful, sturdy body

Large paws

SEEN IT?

MY OBSERVATIONS

Date:

Age (if known):

Colour of fur:

Special markings/features:

Behaviour:

Chow Chows must always be a solid colour, such as black, not parti-coloured (a coat of two or more colours.) This breed has thick fur and the dogs benefit from a monthly bath.

MY DRAWINGS AND PHOTOS

I saw this dog: at home ◯   in a park ◯

Chow Chow

This is an old breed that was probably developed in Mongolia and China. Chow Chows were used as guard and hunting dogs, but are now kept as family pets. These dogs have a reputation for being bad-tempered. However, they can behave very well if they are treated with respect and spend time with strangers and children from an early age. Chow Chows need to be groomed every day.

HEIGHT 46–56 cm

COLOUR Red, black, blue, fawn, white or cream

CHARACTERISTICS Aloof and stubborn

SPECIAL FEATURE Blue-black tongue

Dark eyes

Broad, short muzzle

Tail is curled over body

Blue-black tongue

Deep chest

Short, compact, square-shaped body

Very thick fur

SEEN IT?

MY OBSERVATIONS

Date: _____

Age (if known): _____

Colour of fur: _____

_____

Special markings/features: _____

_____

_____

Behaviour: _____

_____

_____

Newborn Dalmatians are white all over. As the puppies grow their spots appear and become darker. Up to 15 puppies can be born in a single litter.

MY DRAWINGS AND PHOTOS

I saw this dog: at home ◯   in a park ◯

Dalmatian

This is one of the oldest breeds of dogs. Their spotted coats make Dalmatians instantly recognizable and much-loved. They used to run alongside carriages and were admired for their athletic beauty, as well as their ability to guard their owners. Dalmatians have delightful personalities and are full of fun-loving energy. They are loyal and love to be praised by their owners.

HEIGHT 56–61 cm

COLOUR White with black or brown spots

CHARACTERISTICS Outgoing and loyal

SPECIAL FEATURE Spotted coat

Eyes are amber or dark

Ears are set high on the head

Level back

Long tail has an upward curve

Intelligent, lively expression

Strong, square body

Short, neat coat

Round paws

SEEN IT?

in the street ◯   at a dog show ◯   on TV/in a film ◯

MY OBSERVATIONS

Date:
_____

Age (if known):
_____

Colour of fur:
_____
_____

Special markings/features:
_____
_____
_____

Behaviour:
_____
_____
_____

Lhasa Apsos are often treated to a haircut in the summer. Short hair is easier to care for and this practical style is called a 'puppy cut'.

MY DRAWINGS AND PHOTOS

I saw this dog: at home ◯   in a park ◯

Lhasa Apso

These dogs were bred in Tibet to work as watchdogs. They needed long, thick coats to protect them from the cold winters. Today, Lhasa Apsos are most admired for their beautiful coats, which need to be groomed every day to avoid matting. They are intelligent and loyal to their owners, but sometimes dislike strangers. Lhasa Apsos enjoy being with children, but they are upset by loud noises.

HEIGHT 23–28 cm

COLOUR Usually gold to grey

CHARACTERISTICS Trustful and intelligent

SPECIAL FEATURE Healthy and long-lived

Slender head with hair falling over the eyes

Large, fluffy ears

Long back

Long-haired tail is set high and falls over the back

Long beard

Short legs

SEEN IT?

MY OBSERVATIONS

Date:

Age (if known):

Colour of fur:

Special markings/features:

Behaviour:

Poodles that compete in shows have to be regularly groomed, and clipped every six to eight weeks. This fancy style is called the 'continental clip'.

MY DRAWINGS AND PHOTOS

I saw this dog: at home ◯   in a park ◯

Poodle

The Standard Poodle is known for its intelligence and obedience. In the past, Poodles were sometimes used as hunting dogs, but they have been kept as family pets for a long time. Their very dense fur does not shed, so it is often clipped. Standard Poodles have been bred to develop two more types - Miniature and Toy Poodles. All types are good companion dogs, with patient and friendly natures.

HEIGHT 38 cm minimum

COLOUR Black, brown, red, white, tan, blue, grey and mixed colours

CHARACTERISTICS Lively and happy

SPECIAL FEATURE Curly fur

Proud, well-shaped head and face

Short back

Long ears

Fur is normally clipped

Elegant, slender body

Small, oval paws

SEEN IT?

MY OBSERVATIONS

Date: _____

Age (if known): _____

Colour of fur: _____

_____

Special markings/features: _____

_____

_____

Behaviour: _____

_____

_____

Between four and six puppies are usually born in a litter of Shar Peis. Their fur must all be of a solid colour, but puppies from one litter can be different colours.

MY DRAWINGS AND PHOTOS

I saw this dog: at home ◯   in a park ◯

Shar Pei

First bred in China, this breed nearly died out. Shar Peis have become more popular recently, although they can be difficult to care for. Puppies have wrinkled skin, and although some wrinkles disappear as they grow, the adult dogs still have deep folds of skin around their faces and necks. They often have skin and eye problems. Shar Peis are stubborn dogs. They can be difficult to train and may be bad-tempered.

HEIGHT 46–51 cm

COLOUR Black, red, fawn or cream

CHARACTERISTICS Playful and stubborn

SPECIAL FEATURE Wrinkled skin

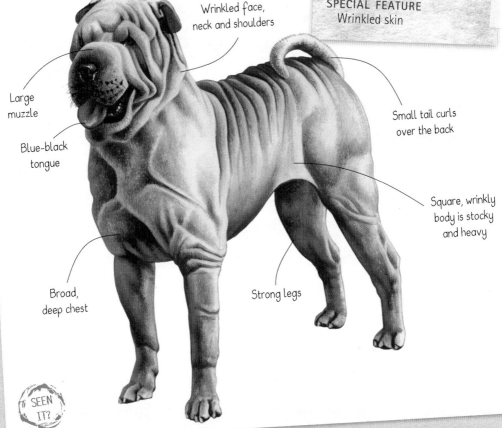

Wrinkled face, neck and shoulders

Large muzzle

Blue-black tongue

Small tail curls over the back

Square, wrinkly body is stocky and heavy

Broad, deep chest

Strong legs

SEEN IT?

MY OBSERVATIONS

Date: _____

Age (if known): _____

Colour of fur: _____

_____

Special markings/features: _____

_____

_____

Behaviour: _____

_____

_____

After a playful romp outdoors, a Shih Tzu's fur can get messy – especially its moustache and beard. However, it needs exercise to avoid getting fat.

MY DRAWINGS AND PHOTOS

I saw this dog: at home ○   in a park ○

Shih Tzu

First bred in Tibet, Shih Tzu dogs have probably been mixed with Pekingese in the past. They are kept as companion dogs and also to show in competitions. Their long, thick fur needs a lot of grooming to keep it in good condition. Shih Tzus are clever dogs that like to play. However, training them is difficult because they are stubborn and do not always like doing what they are told.

HEIGHT 23–27 cm

COLOUR Black, red, grey, gold, brown, silver

CHARACTERISTICS
Independent and clever

SPECIAL FEATURE
Long fringe

Fur may be tied back above eyes

Long, sturdy, small-framed body

Tail is carried over the back

Short, strong legs

Long fur often has white markings

SEEN IT?

MY OBSERVATIONS

Date:

Age (if known):

Colour of fur:

Special markings/features:

Behaviour:

A Border Collie learns to follow a shepherd's instructions and move flocks of sheep around a farm. The shepherd uses a combination of whistles and calls to instruct the dog.

MY DRAWINGS AND PHOTOS

I saw this dog: at home ◯   in a park ◯

Border Collie

These dogs are often found on farms, helping farmers to herd their sheep or cattle. Border Collies are incredibly intelligent and can be trained to follow commands. They are obedient by nature, so they have also been trained to work with rescue parties and as sniffer dogs. Border Collies are energetic and fast, so they need plenty of exercise.

HEIGHT 51–56 cm

COLOUR Black and white

CHARACTERISTICS Intelligent and active

SPECIAL FEATURE Obedient farm dog

Agile, athletic body

White markings

Alert, intelligent expression

Coat is smooth and long

Legs are short for the body length

Oval-shaped paws

SEEN IT?

in the street ◯   at a dog show ◯   on TV/in a film ◯

MY OBSERVATIONS

Date: _____

Age (if known): _____

Colour of fur: _____

_____

Special markings/features: _____

_____

_____

Behaviour: _____

_____

_____

White Boxers are rare and sometimes deaf. Boxers often drool and snore, and can suffer from back and knee problems. They do not like to be too hot or too cold.

MY DRAWINGS AND PHOTOS

I saw this dog: at home ◯   in a park ◯

Boxer

Large, fearless Boxers were bred to be hunting and guard dogs. They are now kept as family pets, but will still guard their owners and their homes with courage. Boxers are energetic dogs and require daily exercise. They also have big appetites and need plenty of good food. Despite their size, Boxers are playful dogs and enjoy being kept busy.

HEIGHT 57–63 cm

COLOUR Red, fawn, brown or white

CHARACTERISTICS Lively and bold

SPECIAL FEATURE Wrinkled face

Muscular, powerful body

Strong chin

Thick tail

Wrinkles around the muzzle

Short-haired coat

Deep chest

SEEN IT?

MY OBSERVATIONS

Date:
_____

Age (if known):
_____

Colour of fur:
_____
_____

Special markings/features:
_____
_____
_____

Behaviour:
_____
_____
_____

A Dobermann's obedient personality suits the skills needed to take part in competitions, and to train as a tracking dog, a police dog or a guard dog.

MY DRAWINGS AND PHOTOS

I saw this dog: at home ◯   in a park ◯

Dobermann

These dogs were bred to be guard dogs. It is thought that many different breeds contributed to the Dobermann, including German Shepherds, Great Danes, Greyhounds and terriers. As a result, Dobermanns combine strength, power and loyalty, as well as beauty and elegance. They are faithful and clever, but extremely energetic and require plenty of exercise, food and careful handling.

HEIGHT 63–72 cm

COLOUR Black with tan markings

CHARACTERISTICS Intelligent and affectionate

SPECIAL FEATURE Often has large litters

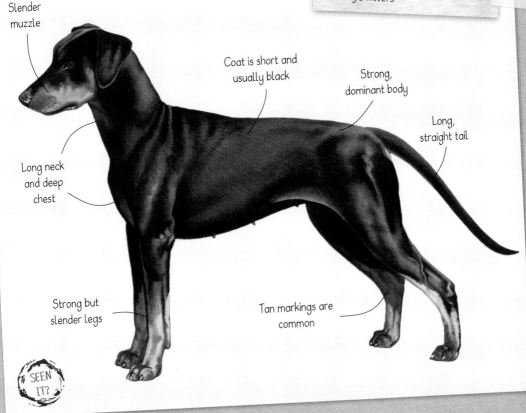

Slender muzzle

Coat is short and usually black

Strong, dominant body

Long, straight tail

Long neck and deep chest

Strong but slender legs

Tan markings are common

SEEN IT?

MY OBSERVATIONS

Date: _____

Age (if known): _____

Colour of fur: _____
_____

Special markings/features: _____
_____
_____

Behaviour: _____
_____
_____

MY DRAWINGS AND PHOTOS

White German Shepherds are a new and popular variety. Some dog clubs treat white German Shepherds as a new breed (called the American White Shepherd).

I saw this dog: at home ◯   in a park ◯

German Shepherd Dog

Also known as Alsatians, German Shepherds are one of the most popular and recognizable breeds of dog. They are loved as family pets, but also work for the police as guard or rescue dogs, and often train as assistance dogs. Intelligent and obedient, German Shepherds are fast learners and form close bonds with their owners.

HEIGHT 55–65 cm

COLOUR Black, or black with tan markings

CHARACTERISTICS Obedient

SPECIAL FEATURE Intelligent working dog

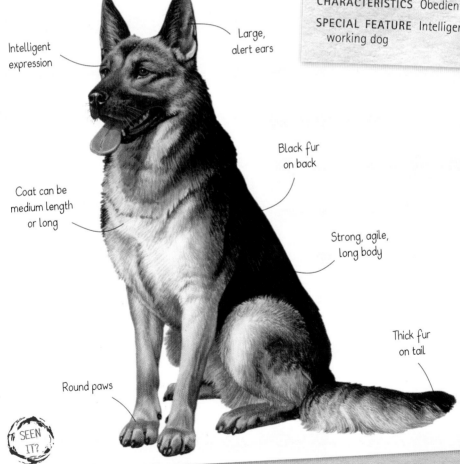

Intelligent expression

Large, alert ears

Black fur on back

Coat can be medium length or long

Strong, agile, long body

Thick fur on tail

Round paws

SEEN IT?

MY OBSERVATIONS

Date:

Age (if known):

Colour of fur:

Special markings/features:

Behaviour:

Handling a Great Dane takes skill and experience. These dogs are powerful but co-operative, which means they are suitable for dog shows and competitions.

MY DRAWINGS AND PHOTOS

I saw this dog: at home ◯   in a park ◯

Great Dane

Developed for hunting large animals, Great Danes have huge, muscular bodies. Today they are used as guard dogs and are family pets. However, their enormous size means they need homes where there is plenty of space and opportunity to exercise. Great Danes are loyal and friendly, and enjoy being around children. Like other big dogs, Great Danes should not have too much exercise while they are growing.

HEIGHT 71 cm minimum

COLOUR Brown, fawn, blue, black, or white with dark patches

CHARACTERISTICS Lively and friendly

SPECIAL FEATURE A good guard dog

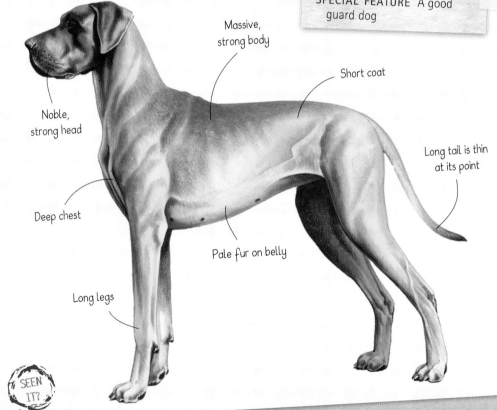

Massive, strong body

Short coat

Noble, strong head

Long tail is thin at its point

Deep chest

Pale fur on belly

Long legs

SEEN IT?

in the street ◯   at a dog show ◯   on TV/in a film ◯

MY OBSERVATIONS

Date: _____

Age (if known): _____

Colour of fur: _____

_____

Special markings/features: _____

_____

_____

Behaviour: _____

_____

_____

Hungarian Pulis were first bred to look after sheep, but they could sometimes be mistaken for one of them! Lively and active, these dogs are lots of fun.

MY DRAWINGS AND PHOTOS

I saw this dog: at home O in a park O

Hungarian Puli

Despite their distinctive appearance, Pulis were bred as working dogs. They needed thick, warm coats to live and work in the cold outdoors, where they herded sheep. Today, the Puli coat is a great attraction, but owners have to devote lots of time to combing it, to prevent the fur becoming knotted. Pulis are friendly and well-behaved.

HEIGHT 37–44 cm

COLOUR Black, grey, fawn or apricot

CHARACTERISTICS Obedient and affectionate

SPECIAL FEATURE Can be used as a sheep dog

Ears are hidden by fur

Stocky body is hidden beneath the coat

Tail is carried over the back

Short, round paws

SEEN IT?

Thick fur forms cords

MY OBSERVATIONS

Date:
_____

Age (if known):
_____

Colour of fur:
_____

_____

Special markings/features:
_____

_____

_____

Behaviour:
_____

_____

_____

Like many breeds, Old English Sheepdogs adore water and love to swim. Unfortunately, it takes a long time for their fur to dry, even after a good shake.

MY DRAWINGS AND PHOTOS

I saw this dog: at home ◯   in a park ◯

Old English Sheepdog

Like most working dogs, Old English Sheepdogs have strong personalities. They can be very loyal and good-tempered, but may also be quick to snap or bark if teased. This large breed was first developed to herd sheep, but is now popular as a pet and a show dog. Its thick, fluffy coat is very attractive, but it requires a lot of grooming to stop it becoming matted.

HEIGHT 56–71 cm

COLOUR Grey or blue, often with white markings

CHARACTERISTICS Excitable and cheerful

SPECIAL FEATURE Thick, shaggy coat

Eyes are often hidden behind fur

Small ears are hidden beneath fur

Thickset, sturdy body

Strong jaws

Long, fluffy fur

Creamy-white fur on chest

Muscular legs

SEEN IT?

MY OBSERVATIONS

Date:
_____

Age (if known):
_____

Colour of fur:
_____
_____

Special markings/features:
_____
_____
_____

Behaviour:
_____
_____
_____

Cardigan Welsh Corgis have longer bodies, larger ears and slightly rounder heads than Pembrokes. They are obedient dogs with loving personalities.

MY DRAWINGS AND PHOTOS

I saw this dog: at home ◯   in a park ◯

Pembroke Welsh Corgi

Once known for having short tempers and nipping people, today, Corgis are friendly dogs that are interested in the world around them and enjoy being with people. They were first bred to herd cattle, and still need plenty of time outdoors. Corgis should be trained to learn obedience and patience. Like other short-legged dogs, Corgis do not like climbing stairs, as it can cause them back pain.

HEIGHT 25–30 cm

COLOUR Usually orange or red
 with white markings

CHARACTERISTICS
 Energetic

SPECIAL FEATURE
 Very short legs

Large,
erect ears

Alert expression

Medium-length fur

Thick, fluffy tail

White fur on
chest

Short legs
with oval paws

SEEN
IT?

MY OBSERVATIONS

Date: _____

Age (if known): _____

Colour of fur: _____

_____

Special markings/features: _____

_____

_____

Behaviour: _____

_____

_____

These dogs tend to drool, especially after eating or drinking. They need special care as they can suffer from sore eyes and do not like the heat.

MY DRAWINGS AND PHOTOS

I saw this dog: at home O in a park O

Saint Bernard

Large Saint Bernards were used as herding and rescue dogs. They became especially famous for their work in the snowy Alps, where they were used to find travellers who had become lost. Today, Saint Bernards are mostly kept as pets, even though they are huge. Many Saint Bernards only live to the age of six or seven years. These massive dogs can be hard to handle, although they have sweet natures.

HEIGHT Up to 91 cm

COLOUR Orange, red, tan with white markings

CHARACTERISTICS Trusting

SPECIAL FEATURE Can be used in search and rescue

Large nose and muzzle

Drooping lips can lead to drooling

Enormous, heavy body

Red markings on white fur

Long, thick neck

Medium-length coat

Strong legs

Large paws

SEEN IT?

Glossary

Amber This honey-yellow colour is used to describe some dogs' eyes.

Assistance dog These dogs can be trained to work with people who need help with practical tasks, such as crossing the road.

Breed Dogs belonging to a particular breed are similar in appearance and often have similar personalities.

Blue Used to describe steel-grey fur that appears to have a blue colour.

Companion dog These breeds are kept just to be pets, or companions, to their owners. They are usually very friendly, are small enough to carry and make good family pets.

Fawn Light yellowish-brown fur may be described as fawn.

Feathering Long hair that grows around the ankles and feet.

Fox hunting A traditional country pastime that involves chasing foxes on horseback, using a pack of hounds to follow the foxes' scent.

Groom To brush a dog's fur and keep it looking glossy and clean.

Guard dog These dogs tend to bark at strangers. They like to protect their homes and owners.

Hound A breed of dog that has been developed to hunt and has a good sense of smell.

Litter A female dog can give birth to a number of puppies at a time. The collective term is a litter.

Matted Fur that has become knotted or tangled.

Muzzle The long nose and mouth of a dog.

Pack animal Some animals like to live in groups called packs. Wild dogs are pack animals and some breeds of dog are pack animals too.

Red Fur that is a vibrant reddish-brown is described as red.

Rescue dog These dogs are trained to help find people using smell and sound. They can find people trapped by avalanches or collapsed buildings.

Show dog A dog kept to compete in dog shows or other competitions.

Sniffer dog These dogs have an exceptionally good sense of smell. They are used to find drugs, food, explosives or other substances.

Spaniel Breeds with long silky coats and drooping ears.

Tan This is a golden-brown colour that is sometimes used to describe dogs' fur.

Terrier These are breeds of small dogs that were developed to drive foxes and other small animals out of their burrows.